JOURNAL OF LIEUT.-COL. ADAM HUBLEY

by Adam Hubley

excerpted from

Journals of the Military Expedition of Major General John Sullivan Against the Six Nations of Indians in 1779 with Records of Centennial Celebration

by Frederick Cook, Secretary of State, 1887

Reprinted by New York History Review

2019

Journal of Lieut.-Col. Adam Hubley
Excerpted from *Journals of the Military Expedition of Major General John Sullivan against the Six Nations of Indians in 1779* by Frederick Cook. Contributed by Thomas R. Bard.

Copyright ©2019 New York History Review. Some rights reserved.

Printed in the United States of America
First Edition

ISBN: 978-1-950822-05-8

To Newtown

Journal of Lieutenant Colonel Adam Hubley

†

JOURNAL OF LIEUT.-COL. ADAM HUBLEY

Adam Hubley, Lieutenant Colonel commanding the Eleventh Pennsylvania Regiment. Published in the appendix of Miner's History of Wyoming. The original contained several illustrations, and maps, not in the published copy. The following is a reprint. This journal has also been republished in Pennsylvania Archives, New Series, Vol. XI. or Vol. II of the Revolution.

Adam Hubley was commissioned as First Lieutenant in the 1st Pa. Battalion, Oct. 27, 177 ; promoted Major of one of the additional regiments in 1776; Lieutenant Colonel, 10th Pa. Reg't, March 12, 1777, ranking from Oct. 4, 1776 ; Lieut. Colonel Commandant 11th Pa. Reg't June 5, 1779 to rank from Feb'y 13, 1779 ; retired Jan'y 1, 1781 ; appointed one of the auctioneers of Philadelphia, and died there of yellow fever in 1793.

Journal of Lieutenant Colonel Adam Hubley

JOURNAL.
GENERAL ORDERS.

Head Quarters, Easton, May 24, A. D., 1779.
When the army shall be fully assembled the following arrangements are to take place: —

Light corps, commanded by Gen. Hand, to consist of — Armandt's, Hubley's, Shott's, 6 companies of Rangers, Wm. Butler's battalion, Morgan's corps, and all volunteers who may join the army.

Maxwell's brigade consists of — Dayton, Shreive, Ogden, Spencer, forming fight of first line.

Poor's brigade consists of — Cilley; Reed, Scammel, Courtland, and form left of first line. Livingston, Dubois, Gainsworth, Olden, and form second line or reserve.

The right of the first line to be covered by 100 men, draughted from Maxwell's brigade, the left to be covered by 100 men detached from Poor's brigade, each flank of the second line to be covered by 50 men detached from Clinton's brigade, the flanking division on the right to consist of Hubley's regiment, and a draught from the line of 100 men, the flanking division on left to consist of the German battalion, and 100 draughted men from the line.

The light corps will advance by the right of companies in files, and keep at least one mile in front. Maxwell's brigade will advance by its right in files, sections, or platoons, as the country will admit. Poor's brigade will advance by its left in the same manner. Clinton's brigade will advance by the right of regiment, in platoons, files, or sections, as the country will admit. All the covering parties and flanking divisions on the right will advance by their left; those on the left of the army will advance by their right. The artillery and pack horses are to march in the centre.

Should the army be attacked in front while on its march, the light corps will immediately form to repulse the enemy, the flanking divisions will endeavor to gain the flanks and rear of the enemy. While the line is forming the pack horses will, in all cases, fall into the position represented on the annexed plan. Should the enemy attack on either flank, the flanking division attacked will form a front, and sustain the attack till reinforced — in which case a part of the light corps is to be immediately detached to gain the enemy's flank and rear, the covering parties of the 2d line to move to gain the other flank. Should the enemy attack our rear, the 2d line will face and form a front to the enemy, the covering parties of the first line will move to sustain it, while the flanking division face about and endeavor to gain their flank and rear. Should the light troops be driven back, they will pass through the intervals of the main army, and form in the rear. Should the enemy in an engagement with the army, when formed, endeavor either flank, the covering party will move up to lengthen the line, and so much as may be found necessary from the flanking division will display outwards to prevent the attempt from succeeding. The light corps will have their advance and flank guards at a good distance from their main body. The flanking division will furnish flank guards, and the 2d line a rear guard for the main army.

When we find that the light corps are engaged in front, the front of the pack horses halt, and the rear close up, while the columns move in a proper distance, close and display, which will bring the horses in the position they are on the plan for the order of battle. Should the attack be made on either, in flank or in rear, the horses must be kept in the position they are at the commencement of the attack, unless other orders are then given.

Journal of Lieutenant Colonel Adam Hubley

SKETCH NO. I.

The trees painted by the Indians, between Owego and Chokunut, on the head waters of the Susquehanna, with their characters.

Wyoming, July 30th, 1779. — Wyoming is situated on the east side of the east branch of the Susquehanna, the town consisting of about seventy houses, chiefly log buildings; besides these buildings there are sundry larger ones which were erected by the army for the purpose of receiving stores, &c., a large bake and smoke houses.

There is likewise a small fort erected in the town, with a strong abatta around it, and a small redoubt to shelter the inhabitants in cases of an alarm. This fort is garrisoned by 100 men, draughted from the western army, and put under the command of Col. Zeb'n Butler. I cannot omit taking notice of the poor inhabitants of the town; two-thirds of them are widows and orphans, who, by the vile hands of the savages, have not only deprived some of tender husbands, some of indulgent parents, and others of affectionate friends and acquaintances, besides robbed and plundered of all their furniture and clothing. In short, they are left totally dependent on the public, and are become absolute objects of charity.

The situation of this place is elegant and delightful. It composes an extensive valley, bounded both on the east and west side of the river by large chains of mountains. The valley, a mere garden, of an excellent rich soil, abounding with large timber of all kinds, and through the center the east branch of the Susquehanna.

NO. 2. A SKETCH OF THE ENCAMPMENT At WYOMING.

Wyoming, July 31st, 1779. — Agreeable to orders, marched the western army under the command of Major General Sullivan, in the following order, from this place to Tioga.

NO. 3. ORDER OF MARCH.

The array being composed of the following regiments and brigades in following manner, viz.; —

Gen. Hand's Brigade, Hubley, German ⋗Regiments, Shott, Spaulding ⋗Ind Corps ⋗ Compose Light Corp

Gen, Maxwell's brigade, Dayton, Shreeve, Ogden, Spencer from main body.

Gen. Poor's brigade, Cilley, Reed, Scammel, Courtland

Took up the line of march about one o'clock, P. M., viz.; light corps advanced in front of main body about a mile; vanguard, consisting of twenty-four men, under command of a subaltern, and Poor's brigade, (main body,) followed by pack horses and cattle, after which one complete regiment, taken alternately from Maxwell's and Poor's brigade, (composed the rear guard.)

Observed the country to be much broken and mountainous, wood chiefly low, and composed of pine only. I was struck on this day's march with the ruins of many houses, chiefly built of logs, and uninhabited; though poor, yet happy in their situation, until that horrid engagement, when the British tyrant let loose upon them his emissaries, the savages of the wood, who not only destroyed and laid waste those cottages, but in cool blood massacred and cut off the inhabitants, not even sparing gray locks or helpless infancy.

About 4 o'clock, P. M., arrived at a most beautiful plain, covered with an abundance of grass, soil excessively rich, through which run a delightful stream of water, known by the name of Lackawanna; crossed the same, and encamped about one mile on the northern side of it, advanced about one half mile in front of main body: after night fell in with rain — continued until morning.

Distance of march this day, 10 miles.

NO. 4. SKETCH OF THE ENCAMPMENT AT LACKAWANNA.

Sunday, August 1st. — Continued at Lackawanna waiting for the fleet, which, by reason of considerable rapids, was detained until nearly 12 o'clock this day before the van could possibly cross there. In getting through, lost two boats, chief of their cargoes were saved. About 2 o'clock, P. M., the whole arrived opposite our encampment, in consequence of which received orders for a march, struck tents accordingly, and moved about 2 o'clock, P. M. About one mile from the encampment, entered the narrows on the river, first detachment and left column under command of Capt. Burk, to join the right column of light corps, and cross the mountain, which was almost inaccessible, in order to cover the army from falling in an ambuscade. Whilst passing through the defile found passage through exceeding difficult and troublesome, owing to the badness of the path; we passed by a most beautiful cataract called the Spring Falls. To attempt a description of it would be almost presumption. Let this short account thereof suffice. The first or upper fall thereof is nearly ninety feet perpendicular, pouring from a solid rock, uttering forth a most beautiful echo, and is received by a cleft of rocks considerably more projected than the former, from whence it rolls gradually and empties into the Susquehanna. Light corps passed and got through the defile about 6 o'clock, P. M; arrived about dusk at a place called Quilutimunk, and encamped one mile in front of the place, occupied that night by the main army.

The main army, on account of the difficult passage, marched nearly all night before they reached their encamping ground. Great quantities of baggage being dropped and left lying that night obliged us to continue on this ground. All the preceding day numbers of our pack horses were sent back and employed in bringing on the scattered stores, &c.; ditance of march this day about 7 miles; fine clear evening. Quilutimunk is a spot of ground situate on the river; fine, open and clear; quantity, about 1200 acres; soil very rich, timber fine, grass in abundance, and contains several exceedingly fine springs.

Journal of Lieutenant Colonel Adam Hubley

SKETCH OF THE ENCAMPMENT AT QUILUTIMUNK.

Monday, August 2d. — In consequence of the difficult and tedious march the preceding day, the army received orders to continue on the ground this day, in the meantime to provide themselves with five days provision, and getting every other matter in perfect readiness for a march next morning at 6 o'clock. Nothing material happened during our stay on this ground.

Wednesday, 3d, — Agreeable to orders took up the line of march at 6 o'clock, A. M. Took the mountains after we assembled — found them exceedingly level for at least six miles. Land tolerable, the timber, viz., pine and white oak, chiefly large. About three miles from Quilutimunk we crossed near another cataract, which descended the mountain in three successive falls, the least of which is equal if not superior to the one already described. Although it is not quite so high, it is much wider, and likewise empties into the Susquehanna, seemingly white as milk. They are commonly known by the name of Buttermilk Falls.

SKETCH OF BUTTERMILK FALLS.

About 12 o'clock we descended the mountains near the river; marched about one mile on flat piece of ground, and arrived at Tunkhannunk, a beautiful stream of water so called, which empties into the Susquehanna; crossed the same, and encamped on the river about 1 o'clock, P. M. Nothing material happened this day excepting a discovery of two Indians by the party on the west side of the river. Indians finding themselves rather near the party were obliged to leave their canoe, and make through the mountains. Party took possession of the canoe, and brought it to their encamping place, for that evening immediately opposite the main army. Distance of march this day, 12 miles.

SKETCH OF TUNKHANNUNK ENCAMPMENT.

Wednesday 4th - The army was in motion 5 o'clock, A. M., and moved up the river for three miles, chiefly on the beach, close under an almost inaccessible mountain. We then ascended the same with the greatest difficulty, and continued on it for near seven miles. A considerable distance from the river the path along the mountain was exceedingly rough, and carried through several very considerable swamps, in which were large morasses. The land in general thin and broken, abounds in wild deer and other game. We then descended the mountain, and at the foot of it crossed a small creek called Massasppi, immediately where it empties into the river. We then continued up the same until we made Vanderlip's farm, discovered several old Indian encampments; one of them appeared to have been very large.

The land, after crossing Massasppi, was exceedingly fine and rich, the soil very black and well timbered, chiefly with black walnut, which are remarkably large, some not less than six feet over, and excessively high. It is likewise well calculated for making fine and extensive meadows. The main army took post for this night on Vanderlip's farm, and the infantry advanced about one mile higher up, and encamped about 1 o'clock, P. M., on a place known by the name of Williamson's farm. Distance of march this day, 14 miles; fine clear day, very hot.

SKETCH OF THE ENCAMPMENT, VANDERLIP'S AND WILLIAMSON'S FARM.

Thursday 5th. — In consequence of orders issued last evening to march this morning at 5 o'clock, we struck tents and loaded baggage. But the boats being considerably impeded by the rapidness of the water some miles below our encampment, could not reach us, and we were obliged to halt all night. Did not join us until 9 o'clock, A. M., all which time we were obliged to halt. On their arrival the whole army was put in motion, and as more danger on this day's march was apprehended than any before, the following distribution of the army took place, viz.: The right and left columns of the light corps, conducted by Gen. Hand, moved along the top of a very high mountain; main body of light corps, under Col. Hubley's command, with an advance of twenty-four men, moved on the beach several miles on the edge of the water. The main army, followed by the baggage, &c., flanked on their right by four hundred men, who had likewise to take this mountain. Thus, we moved for several miles, then arrived in a small valley called Depue's farm; the land very good. Observed and reconnoitered this ground for some distance, it being the place on which Col. Hartley was attacked by the savages last year, on his return from Tioga to Wyoming. The country being fine and open, some loss was sustained on both sides; the savages at last gave way, and Col. Hartley pursued his route to Wyoming without further molestation. Continued our march for about one mile, and formed a junction with the parties on the right flank, ascended a high mountain, and marched for some miles on the same. Land poor, timber but small, chiefly pine, after which descended the mountain nearly one mile in length, and arrived in a fine and large valley, known by the name of Wyalusing. The main army took post at this place, and the infantry advanced about one mile in front of them, and encamped about 2 o'clock, P. M. Clear but very warm day; distance of march this day, 10 miles.

This valley was formerly called Oldman's farm, occupied by the Indians and white people; together, they had about sixty houses, a considerable Moravian meeting house, and sundry other public buildings; but since the commencement of the present war the whole has been consumed and laid waste, partly by the savages and partly by our own people. The land is extraordinarily calculated chiefly for meadows. The grass at this time is almost beyond description, high and thick, chiefly blue grass, and the soil of the land very rich. The valley contains about 1200 acres of land, bounded on one side by an almost inaccessible mountain, and on the other by the river Susquehanna.

SKETCH OF THE ENCAMPMENT AT WYALUSING.

Friday, Aug. 6th. — The boats not arriving before late this day, the army received orders to continue on the ground. In the meantime to be provided with three days provision, get their arms and accoutrements in perfect order, and be in readiness for a march early to-morrow morning. A sub. and twenty-four men from my regiment reconnoitered vicinity of camp; returned in the evening ; made no discoveries. Rain all night.

Saturday 7th. — The heavy rain last night and this morning rendered it utterly impossible to march this day; continued on the ground for further orders.

A captain and thirty men from my regiment reconnoitered vicinity of camp; made no discoveries.

This day received a letter (by express) from his Excellency Gen. Washington, dated Head Quarters, at New Windsor.

Sunday, 8th. — The army moved (in same order as on 5th) this morning at 5 o'clock; crossed Wyalusing creek, and ascended an extensive mountain, the top remarkably level;

land poor, and timber small. Arrived about 10 o'clock, A. M., at the north end, and descended the same close on the river side, and continued along the beach for some distance, after which we entered an extensive valley or plain, known by the name of Standing Stone; made a halt here for about half an hour for refreshments. This place derives its name from a large stone standing erect in the river immediately opposite this plain. It is near twenty feet in height, fourteen feet in width, and three feet in depth. This valley abounds in grass, the land exceedingly fine, and produces chiefly white oak, black walnut, and pine timber. After refreshment continued our march along the same valley; land not quite so fine. Arrived about 3 o'clock, P. M., at a small creek called Wesauking; crossed the same, and encamped about one mile beyond it, and immediately on the river.

Four o'clock, P. M. — Since our arrival at this place some of my officers discovered a small Indian encampment, seemingly occupied but a few days since; found near the same a neat canoe, which they brought off. This morning the scout, (of three men,) sent up to Sheshequin some days since, returned without making any discoveries.

General Sullivan, on account of his indisposition, came on in the boat.

SKETCH OF STANDING STONE.
SKETCH OF ENCAMPMEMT AT WESAUKING.

Monday, August 9th. — The boats not being able to reach Wesauking, the ground on which light corps encamped preceding evening. The main body in consequence thereof took post and encamped at Standing Stone, about three miles below light corps encampment, for protection of the boats.

The light corps, on account of their detached situation from main body the preceding evening, and apprehending some danger, being considerably advanced in the enemy's country, for their greater security stood under arms from 3 o'clock, A. M., until daylight, where they dismissed, with orders to hold themselves in readiness at a moment's warning. Previous to their dismissal my light infantry was sent out to reconnoitre the vicinity of encampment; returned about 7 o'clock, A. M. — made no discovery.

This morning, 9 o'clock, boats hove in sight, in consequence thereof received orders to strike tents, and be in readiness for a march; main army in the meantime arrived about 10 o'clock; the whole was in motion, marched through a difficult swamp; at north of same crossed a small stream, and ascended a hill; lands poor, and wood but indifferent. About 12 o'clock, P. M., descended the same, and entered a small valley; continued about half mile, when we ascended a very remarkable high mountain, generally known by the name of Break Neck Hill.

This mountain derives its name from the great height, of the difficult and narrow passage, not more than one foot wide, and remarkable precipice which is immediately perpendicular, and not less than 180 feet deep. One mis-step must inevitably carry you from top to bottom without the least hope or chance of recovery. At north end of same entered a mountainous and beautiful valley called Sheshecununk. General Sullivan, with a number of officers, made a halt here at a most beautiful run of water, took a bite of dinner, and proceeded on along the valley, which very particularly struck my attention. Any quantity of meadow may be made here; abounds with all kinds of wood, particularly white oak, hickory, and black walnut; the ground covered with grass and pea vines; the soil in general very rich. About 4 o'clock, P. M., arrived on the bank of the river; the whole encamped in a line on a most beautiful plain; consists chiefly in meadows, the grass remarkably thick and high. On our arrival here made discoveries of some new Indian tracks, places on which fire had just been, and fresh boughs cut, and appeared as if the place had just been occupied a few hours before our arrival. Distance of march this, day, 9 1/2 miles.

SKETCH OF ENCAMPMENT SHESHECUNUNK.

Tuesday, August 10th. — Set in with rain, and boats not reaching this place before 9 o'clock this morning; army received orders to continue on the ground until further orders. Men drew and cooked two days provisions.

One regiment from each of the brigades attended General Sullivan. The general and field officers of the army whilst they were reconnoitering the river and ground near Tioga branch, about three miles above this place, returned without any discoveries worthy of remark about 4 o'clock, P. M.

Wednesday, August 11th. — Agreeable to orders the army moved this morning at 8 o'clock, A. M., in the usual order, flight corps moved half an hour before the main army, and took post on the banks of the river near the fording place. On the arrival of the main army and boats. Col. Forest drew up his boat at the fording place, and fixed several six pounders on the opposite shore in order to scour the woods and thickets, and prevent any ambuscade from taking place. In the meantime the light corps marched by platoons, linked together, on account of the rapidity of the water, and forded the same, and effected a landing about 9 o'clock ; they immediately advanced about one hundred yards from the river, and formed in line of battle, in order to cover the landing of the main army, which was safely effected about 10 o'clock, A. M., after which came on pack horse's, cattle, &c., covered by a regiment which composed the rear guard. About half past ten o'clock the whole moved in following order.

ORDER OF MARCH UP TIOGA FLATS.

Previous to our arrival on the flats we had to pass about one and a half mile through a dark, difficult swamp, which was covered with weeds and considerable underwood, interspersed with large timber, chiefly buttonwood. We then entered the flats near the place on which Queen Esther's palace stood, and was destroyed by Col. Hartley's detachment last fall. The grass is remarkably thick and high. We continued along the same for about one mile, and arrived at the entrance of Tioga branch into Susquehanna about 1 o'clock; we crossed the same, and landed on a peninsula of land which extends towards Chemung, and is bounded on the east by Susquehanna, and on the west by Tioga branch, and continued up the same for about two miles and a half and encamped. This peninsula is composed of excellent meadow and upland; grass is plenty, and timber of all kinds, and soil in general good; distance of march this day, three miles. Since our arrival a scout of eight men was ordered up to reconnoitre Chemung, and endeavor to make discoveries of the number of savages, and their situation, if possible.

Thursday, August 12th. — Tioga Plain. This being a plain calculated to cover the western army during the expedition to the northern part of it, a garrison for that purpose is to remain until- our return. Sundry works for the security of the same are now erecting about two and a half miles distant from where Tioga branch empties into the Susquehanna, and where the two rivers are about 190 yards distance from each other; those works to extend from river to river.

Captain Cummings with his scout (sent out last evening) returned this day 11 o'clock, A. M.; made several discoveries at Chemung; an Indian village twelve miles distance from this place; in consequence of which a council of war sat, and determined an expedition should immediately take place for the reduction of the same. The array (two regiments excepted) received orders to be in readiness for an immediate march. Eight o'clock, P. M., the whole were in motion, and proceeded for Chemung.

SKETCH ON ENCAMPMENT AND WORKS ON TIOGA PLAINS.

August 13t, 1779. — Eight o'clock, P. M., the army having marched last evening in the following order, viz.: Light corps, under command of Gen. Hand, led the van, then followed Gens. Poor and Maxwell's brigades, which formed main body, and corps de reserve, the whole under the immediate command of Maj. Gen. Sullivan. The night being excessively dark, and the want of proper guides, impeded our march, besides which we had several considerable defiles to march through, that we could not possibly reach Chemung till after daylight. The morning being foggy favoured our enterprise. Our pilot on our arrival, from some disagreeable emotions he felt, could not find the town. We discovered a few huts, which we surrounded, but found them vacated; after about one hour's march we came upon the main town. The following disposition for surprising the same was ordered to take place, viz.. Two regiments, one from the light corps, and one from main body, were ordered to cross the river and prevent the enemy from making their escape that way, should they still hold the town. The remainder of the light corps, viz., two independent companies, and my regiment, under command of Hand, were to make the attack on the town. Gen. Poor was immediately to move up and support the light corps. We moved in this order accordingly, but the savages having probably discovered our scouting party the preceding day, defeated our enterprise by evacuating the village previous to our coming, carrying off with them nearly all their furniture and stock, and leaving an empty village only, which fell an easy conquest about 5 o'clock, A. M. The situation of this village was beautiful; it contained fifty or sixty houses, built of logs and frames, and situate on the banks of Tioga branch, and on a most fertile, beautiful, and extensive plain, the lands chiefly calculated for meadows, and the soil rich.

The army continued for some small space in the town. Gen. Hand, in the meantime, advanced my light infantry company, under Capt. Bush, about one mile beyond the village, on a path which leads to a small Indian habitation, called Newtown. On Capt. Bush's arrival there he discovered fires burning, an Indian dog, which lay asleep, a number of deer skins, some blankets, &c,; he immediately gave information of his discoveries, in consequence of which the remainder part of the light corps, viz.: the two independent companies, and my regiment, under Gen. Hand's command, were ordered to move some miles up the path, and endeavor, if possible, to make some discoveries. We accordingly proceeded on in the following order, viz. Captain Walker, with twenty-four men, composed the van, the eleventh regiment, under my command, after which the two independent companies, the whole covered on the left by Tioga branch, and on the right by Capt. Bush's infantry company of forty men. In this order we moved somewhat better than a mile beyond this place. The first fires were discovered, when our van was fired upon by a party of savages, who lay concealed on a high hill immediately upon our right, and which Capt. Bush had not yet made. We immediately formed a front with my regiment, pushed up the hill with a degree of intrepidity seldom to be met with, and, under a very severe fire from the savages. Capt. Bush, in the meantime, endeavored to gain the enemy's rear. They, seeing the determined resolution of our troops, retreated; and according to custom, previous to our dislodging them, carried off their wounded and dead, by which means they deprived us from coming to the knowledge of their wounded and dead. The ground on the opposite side of the mountain or ridge, on which the action commenced, being composed of swamp or low ground, covered with underwood, &c , favored their retreat, and prevented our pursuing them, by which means they got off.

Our loss on this occasion, which totally (excepting two) fe (sic) on my regiment, was as follows, viz.. two captains, one adjutant, one guide, and eight privates wounded, arid one sergeant, one drummer, and four privates killed. Officers' names : Captain Walker, (slight wound,) Captain Carberry, and Adj. Huston, (I fear mortal.)

After gaining the summit of the hill, and dislodging the enemy, we marched by the right of companies in eight columns, and continued along the same line until the arrival of General Sullivan. We then halted for some little time, and then returned to the village, which was instantly laid in ashes, and a party detached to cross the river to destroy the corn, beans, &c., of which there were several very extensive fields, and those articles in the greatest perfection. Whilst the troops were engaged in this business, Gens. Poor and Maxwell's brigades were fired upon, lost one man, killed, and several wounded. The whole business being completed, we returned to the ruins of the village, halted some little time, and received orders to return to Tioga Plain, at which place we arrived at 8 o'clock, considerably fatigued. Lest the savages should discover our loss, after leaving the place, I had the dead bodies of my regiment carried along, fixed on horses, and brought to this place for interment. The expedition from the first to last continued twenty-four hours, of which time my regiment was employed, without the least intermission, twenty-three hours; the whole of our march not less than forty miles.

Saturday, August 14th. — This morning 10 o'clock, A. M., had the bodies of those brave veterans, who so nobly distinguished themselves, and bravely fell in the action of yesterday, interred with military honours, (firing excepted.) Parson Rogers delivered a small discourse on the occasion.

Was employed greater part of the day in writing to my friends at Lancaster and Philadelphia, which were forwarded the same evening.

Sunday 15th. — Agreeable to orders of yesterday, seven hundred men were ordered to march on the grand parade for inspection, and to be furnished with ammunition and eight days provision, for the purpose of marching up the

Susquehanna and meeting General Clinton, Who is now on his march to form a junction with this army.

Two o'clock, P. M., a firing was heard on the west side of Tioga branch, immediately opposite our encampment. A number of Indians undercover of a high mountain, advanced on a large meadow or flat of ground, on which our cattle and horses were grazing. Unfortunately, two men were there to fetch some horses, one of which was killed and scalped, the other slightly wounded, but got clear. One bullock was likewise killed, and several public horses taken off. My regiment was ordered in pursuit of them; we accordingly crossed the branch and ascended the mountain, marched along the summit of the same for upwards of two miles in order to gain their rear; but the enemy having too much start got clear. After scouring the mountains and valleys near the same, we returned, much fatigued, about 5 o'clock, P. M.

Monday, 16th. — The detachment under General Poor's command, agreeable to orders, moved this day, 1 o'clock, P. M., up the Susquehanna for the purpose of forming a junction with Gen. Clinton.

Several of our out continentals alarmed the camp by firing off several guns about 1 o'clock in the morning, in consequence of which light corps stood under arms. Several patrols were sent out to reconnoitre the front of encampment, returned near day-break, but made no discoveries — alarm proved premature. Gen. Hand, being ordered with the detachment under Gen. Poor, the command of light corps devolved on me during his absence.

Tuesday, 17th. — Seven o'clock, P. M., a firing was heard about five hundred yards immediately in front of light corps' encampment. A party of fifty men was immediately detached to endeavour to find out the cause of it; returned at 8 o'clock, P. M.; reported that a party of Indians, eleven in number, had way-laid a few pack horsemen, who were just returning with their horses from pasture; that they had killed and scalped one man, and wounded another; the wounded man got safe to camp, and the corpse of the other was likewise brought in.

An alarm was fired by a continental about 11 o'clock, P. M. but proved false.

Wednesday, 18th. — In order to entrap some of those savages who keep sneaking about the encampment, the following parties ordered out for that purpose, and to be relieved daily by an equal number until we leave this ground, viz: one subaltern and twenty men on the mountain opposite the encampment; one subaltern and twenty men on the island, about a mile and half above the encampment, on Tioga branch, and one subaltern and twenty men in the woods, about a mile and a half immediately in front of light corps' encampment, with orders to waylay and take every other means to take them.

This day, by particular request of several gentlemen, a discourse was delivered in the Masonic form, by Dr. Rogers, on the death of Captain Davis of the 11th Penn., and Lieutenant Jones of the Delaware regiments, who were, on the 23d of April last, most cruelly and inhumanly massacred and scalped by the savages, emissaries employed by the British king, as they were marching with a detachment for the relief of the garrison at Wyoming.

Those gentlemen were both members of that honourable and ancient Society of Freemen. A number of brethren attended on this occasion in proper form, and the whole was conducted with propriety and harmony. Text preached on this solemn occasion was the first clause in the 7th verse of the 7th chapter of Job, " Remember my life is but wind."

Thursday, 19th. — Nothing remarkable this day.

Friday, 20th. — This day arrived Lieut. Boyd, of Col. Butler's regiment, with accounts of Gen. Clinton's movements on the Susquehanna, and that a junction was formed by him with Gen. Poor's detachment, Chokoanut, about thirty-five miles from this place. Rain very heavy chief part of the day.

Saturday, 21st. — The detachments under Gens. Clinton and Poor, on account of the very heavy rain yesterday, did not reach this encampment as was expected.

Sunday, 22d. — This day, 10 o'clock, A. M., Gens, Clinton and Poor's detachments, with about two hundred and twenty boats, passed light corps' encampment for the main army, about one and a half miles in their rear. On their passing, they were saluted with thirteen rounds from the park ; the light corps being likewise drawn up, and received them in proper form, with Col. Proctor's music, and drums and fifes beating and playing.

Monday, 23d, — This day a most shocking affair happened, by an accident of a gun, which went off, the ball of which entered a tent in which was Capt. Kimball, of Gen. Poor's brigade, and a lieutenant; the captain was unfortunately killed, and the lieutenant wounded.

Gen. Clinton, having formed a junction with the army at this place yesterday, the following alterations in the several brigades were ordered to take place, viz. ; Col. Courtland's regiment to be annexed to General Clinton's, Colonel Older to General Poor's, and Colonel Butler's regiment, with Major Parr's corps, to General Hand's brigade.

Tuesday, 24th. — This day employed hands to make bags for the purpose of carrying flour; hands employed all day and night in this business.

Agreeable to orders a signal gun was fired for the whole army to strike tents, 5 o'clock, P. M., and marched some distance in order to form the line of march. Seven o'clock, P. M., another signal gun was fired for the army to encamp in proper order, and to be in readiness for an immediate march. Col. Butler's regiment, with Major Parr's riflemen, joined light corps, and encamped with them this day, 7 o'clock, V. M.

Colonel Shrieve took command of Fort Sullivan this day agreeable to orders. Flying hospital and stores were moved this day to the garrison.

Wednesday, 25th — This morning was entirely devoted to packing up and getting everything in readiness for an immediate march. A heavy rain fell in at 11 o'clock, continued, greater part of the day, which prevented our movements.

Thursday, 26th — The army not being perfectly ready to march at 8 o'clock, A. M., agreeable to yesterday's orders, the signal gun for a march was not fired until 11 o'clock, when the whole took up the line of march in the following order, namely: Light corps, commanded by General Hand, marched in six columns, the right commanded by Colonel Butler, and the left by myself. Major Parr, with the riflemen, dispersed considerably in front of the whole, with orders to reconnoitre all mountains, defiles, and other suspicious, places, previous to the arrival of the army, to prevent any surprise or ambuscade from taking place. The pioneers, under command of a captain, subaltern, then followed after, which preceded the park of artillery; then came on the main army, in two columns, in the centre of which moved the pack horses and cattle, the whole flanked on right and left by the flanking divisions, commanded by Colonel Dubois and Colonel Ogden, and rear brought up by General Clinton's brigade; in this position the whole moved to the upper end of Tioga flats, about three miles above Fort Sullivan, where we encamped for this night.

This day disposed of one of my horses to Mr. Bond, captain, on account of his indisposition, obtained leave to continue either at Fort Sullivan, or go to Wyoming, until the return of the regiment from the expedition.

Friday, August 27th. — On account of some delays this morning army did not move until half past eight o'clock, A. M. Previous to the march the pioneers, under cover of the rifle corps, were advanced to the first and second defile, or narrows, some miles in front of our encampment, where they were employed in mending and cutting a road for the pack to pass. The army marched in same order of yesterday, the country through which they had to pass being exceedingly mountainous and rough, and the slow movements of the pack considerably impeded the march. About 7 o'clock, P. M., we arrived near the last narrows, at the lower end of Chemung, where we encamped in the following order: Light corps near the entrance of the defile or narrows, and in front of some very extensive corn-fields, some refugee Tories, now acting with the favour of the main army, about one mile in our rear, and immediately fronting the corn-fields. After encamping had an agreeable repast of corn, potatoes, beans, cucumbers, watermelons, squashes, and other vegetables, which were in great plenty, (produced) from the corn-fields already mentioned, and in the greatest perfection; distance of march this day, six miles.

Saturday, August 28th. — Fore part of this day being employed by the general and principal officers of the army in reconnoitering the river and finding out some fording place for the artillery, pack horses, and cattle to cross, to gain Chemung, the defile or narrows mentioned in my yesterday's journal being so excessively narrow, and, indeed, almost impracticable for them to pass.

The following disposition for the marching of the army took place accordingly, namely: The rifle corps, with General Maxwell's brigade, and left flanking division of the army, covering the park, pack horses, and cattle, crossed to the west side of the river, and about one and a half mile above recrossed the same, and formed a junction on the lower end of Chemung flats with the light corps, Generals Poor and Clinton's brigades, and right flanking division of the army, who took their route across an almost inaccessible mountain, on the east side of the river, the bottom of which forms the narrows already mentioned.

The summit was gained with the greatest difficulty; on the top of the mountain the lands, which are level and extensive, are exceedingly rich with large timber, chiefly oak, interspersed with underwood and excellent grass. The prospect from this mountain is most beautiful; we had a view of the country of at least twenty miles round; the fine, extensive plains, interspersed with streams of water, made the prospect pleasing and elegant from this mountain. We observed, at some considerable distance, a number of clouds of smoke arising, where we concluded the enemy to be encamped.

Previous to the movement of the army this day; a small party of men were sent across the river in order to destroy some few Indian huts, which were immediately opposite our encampment. Before the business was quite effected they were fired upon by a party of Indians, who, after giving the fire, immediately retreated; the party executed their orders, and all returned unhurt to the army.

The scout sent out last evening to reconnoitre the enemy near Newtown, (an Indian village so called,) returned this day, and reported they discovered a great number of fires, and that they supposed, from the extensive piece of ground covered by the fires, the enemy must be very formidable, and mean to give us battle. They likewise discovered four or five small scouting parties on their way towards this place, it is supposed to reconnoitre our army. Since our arrival here a great quantity of furniture was found by our soldiers which was concealed in the adjacent woods. After forming the junction above mentioned we took up the line of march, and moved to the upper Chemung town, and encamped about 6 o'clock, P. M., for this night. Distance of march on a straight course, about two miles.

From the great quantities of corn and other vegetables here and in the neighbourhood, it is supposed they intended to establish their principal magazine at this place, which seems to be their chief rendezvous, whenever they intend to go to war; it is the key to the Pennsylvania and New York frontier. The corn already destroyed by our army is not less than 5,000 bushels upon a moderate calculation, and the quantity yet in the ground in this neighborhood, is at least the same, besides which there are vast quantities of beans, potatoes, squashes, pumpkins, &c., which shared the fate of the corn.

Sunday, August 29ih. — This morning at 9 o'clock the army moved in the same order of the 26 ; the riflemen were well scattered in front of the light corps, who moved with the greatest precision and caution. On our arrival near the ridge on which the action of the 13th commenced with light corps, our van discovered several Indians in front, one of whom gave them a fire, and then fled. We continued our march for about one mile; the rifle corps entered a low marshy ground which seemed well calculated for forming ambuscades ; they advanced with great precaution, when several more Indians were discovered who fired and retreated. Major Parr, from those circumstances, judged it rather dangerous to proceed any further without taking every caution to reconnoitre almost every foot of ground, and ordered one of his men to mount a tree and see if he could make any discoveries ; after being some time on the tree he discovered the movements of several Indians, (which were rendered conspicuous by the quantity of paint they had on them,) as they were laying behind an extensive breastwork, which extended at least half a mile, and most artfully covered with green boughs and trees, having their right flank secured by the river, and their left by a mountain. It was situated on a rising ground — about one hundred yards in front of a difficult stream of water, bounded by the marshy ground already mentioned on our side, and on the other, between it and the breastworks, by an open and clear field. Major Parr immediately gave intelligence to General Hand of his discoveries, who immediately advanced the light corps within about three hundred yards of the enemy's works, and formed in line of battle; the rifle corps, under cover, advanced, and lay under the bank of the creek within one hundred yards of the lines. Gen. Sullivan, having previous notice, arrived with the main army, and ordered the following disposition to take place: The rifle and light corps to continue their position; the left flanking division, under command of Colonel Ogden, to take post on the left flank of the light corps, and General Maxwell's brigade, some distance in the rear, as a corps de reserve, and Colonel Proctor's artillery in front of the centre of the light corps, and immediately opposite the breastwork. A heavy fire ensued between the rifle corps and the enemy, but little damage was done on either side. In the meantime. Generals Poor and Clinton's brigades, with the right flanking division, were ordered to march and gain, if possible, the enemy's flank and rear, whilst the rifle and light corps amused them in front. Col. Proctor had orders to be in readiness with his artillery and attack the lines, first allowing a sufficient space of time to Generals Poor, &c., to gain their intended stations. About 3 o'clock, P. M., the artillery began their attack on the enemy's works; the rifle and light corps in the meantime prepared to advance and charge; but the enemy, finding their situation rather precarious, and our troops determined, left and retreated from their works with the greatest precipitation, leaving behind them a number of blankets, gun covers, and kettles, with corn boiling over the fire. Generals Poor, &c., on account of several difficulties which they had to surmount, could not effect their designs, and the enemy probably having intelligence of their approach, posted a number of troops on the top of a mountain, over which they had to advance. On their arrival near the summit of the same, the enemy gave them a fire, and wounded several officers and soldiers. General Poor pushed on and gave them a fire, as they retreated, and killed five of the savages. In course of the day we took nine scalps, (all savages,) and two prisoners, who were separately examined, and gave the following corresponding account: that the enemy were seven hundred men strong, viz, five hundred savages, and two hundred Tories, with about twenty British troops, commanded by a Seneca chief, the two Butlers, Brandt, and M' Donald.

The infantry pushed on towards Newtown; the main army halted and encamped near the place of action, near which were several extensive fields of corn and other vegetables. About six o'clock, P. M., the infantry returned and encamped near the main army.

The prisoners further informed us that the whole of their party had subsisted on corn only for this fortnight past, and that they had no other provisions with them; and that their next place of rendezvous would be at Catharines town, an Indian village about twenty-five miles from this place.

Distance of march (exclusive of counter-marches) this day, about eight miles.

Monday, August 30th. — On account of the great quantities of corn, beans, potatoes, turnips, and other vegetables, in destroying of which the troops were employed, and the rain which set in the after part of the day obliged us to continue on the ground for this day and night. The troops were likewise employed in drawing eight days provisions, (commencing 1st day of September.) The reason of drawing this great quantity at one time was, (however inconsistent with that economy which is absolutely necessary in our present situation, considering the extensive campaign before us, and the time of consequence it will require to complete it,) the want of pack horses for transporting the same, and in order to expedite this great point in view, are obliged to substitute our soldiery for carrying the same.

From the great and unparalleled neglect of those persons employed for the purpose of supplying the western army with everything necessary to enable them to carry through the important expedition required of them. General Sullivan was at this early period under the disagreeable necessity of issuing the following address to the army, which was communicated by the commanding officers to their corps separately, viz.;

GENERAL Sullivan's address.

"The commander-in-chief informs the troops that he used every effort to procure proper supplies for the army, and to obtain a sufficient number of horses to transport them, but owing to the inattention of those whose business it was to make the necessary provision, he failed of obtaining such an ample supply as he wished, and greatly, fears that the supplies on hand will not, without the greatest prudence, enable him to complete the business of the expedition.

He therefore requests the several brigadiers and officers commanding corps to take the mind of the troops under their respective commands, whether they will, whilst in this country, which abounds with corn and vegetables of every kind, be content to draw one half of flour, one half of meat and salt a day. And he desires the troops to give their opinions with freedom and as soon as possible.

Should they generally fall in with the proposal, he promises they shall be paid that part of the rations which is held back at the full value in money."

"He flatters himself that the troops who have discovered

so much bravery and firmness will readily consent to fall in with a measure so essentially necessary to accomplish the important purpose of the expedition, to enable them to add to the laurels they have already gained.

"The enemy have subsisted for a number of days on corn only, without either salt, meat, or flour, and the general cannot persuade himself that troops, who so far surpass them in bravery and true valour, will suffer themselves to be outdone in that fortitude and perseverance, which not only distinguishes but dignifies the soldier. He does not mean to continue this through the campaign, but only wishes it to be adopted in those places where vegetables may supply the place of a part of the common ration of meat and flour, which will be much better than without any.

"The troops will please to consider the matter, and give their opinion as soon as possible."

Agreeable to the above address, the army was drawn up, (this evening,) in corps separately, and the same, through their commanding officers, made known to them, and their opinions requested thereupon, when the whole, without a dissenting voice cheerfully agreed to the request of the general, which they signified by unanimously holding up their hands and giving three cheers.

This remarkable instance of fortitude and virtue cannot but endear those brave troops to all ranks of people, more particularly as it was so generally and cheerfully entered into without a single dissenting voice.

Tuesday, August 31st. — Took up our line of march in usual order at 9 o'clock, A. M. marched about four miles and a half through a broken and mountainous country, and an almost continuous defile on the east side of Cayuga branch, the west of the same for that distance was an excellent plain, on which large quantities of corn, beans, potatoes, and other vegetables stood, and were destroyed by us the preceding day. We then crossed Cayuga branch, where it forks with a stream of water running east and west, and landed on a most beautiful piece of country remarkably level. On the banks of the same stood a small Indian village, which was immediately destroyed. The soldiers found great quantities of furniture, &c., which was buried, some of which they carried off, and some was destroyed. About 2 o'clock, P. M., we proceeded along the path which leads to

Catharines town, (an Indian village,) and leaves the Cayuga branch on its left. About 5 o'clock, P. M., we encamped on a most beautiful plain, interspersed with marshes, well calculated for meadows. Wood chiefly pine, interspersed with hazel brushes, and great quantities of grass; distance of march this day, 10 miles.

Wednesday, September 1st. — About 9 o'clock, P. M., whole army moved in good order on a level piece of ground. About 11 o'clock, A. M., we entered an extensive hemlock swamp, not less than six miles through; the path through almost impassable, owing to the number of defiles, long ranges of mountains, ravine after ravine, interspersed with thick underwood, &c. The infantry, with the greatest difficulty, got through about half past nine o'clock, P. M. The remainder of the army, with the pack horses, cattle, &c., were chiefly the whole night employed in getting through.

As the infantry were approaching Catharines town we were alarmed by the howling of dogs and other great noise. A few of the riflemen were dispatched in order to reconnoitre the place. In the meantime we formed in two solid columns, at fixed bayonets, with positive orders not a man to fire his gun, but to rush on in case the enemy should make a stand;

but the riflemen, who had been sent to reconnoitre the town, returned with the intelligence the enemy had left it. We then immediately altered our position on account of the narrowness of the road, and marched in files through the first part of the town, after which we crossed the creek: in a field immediately opposite, where there stood a number of houses also, where we encamped, and substituted the timber of the houses in room of firewood. On our arrival, we found, a number of fires burning, which appeared as if they had gone off precipitately. This day's march completed 12 miles.

Thursday, Sept. 2d. — The dismal situation of our pack horses and cattle, of which several were killed by falling into ditches, and several otherwise disabled in getting through this horrid swamp last evening, prevented our march this morning. The fore part of this day was entirely employed in collecting them, which, from their scattered and dispersed situation, was attended with the greatest difficulty.

We this morning found an old squaw who, we suppose, by reason of her advanced age, could not be carried off, and therefore was left to our mercy. On examining her she informed us that the Indians, on our approach last evening, went off very precipitately; that the women and children had gone off in the morning to take shelter in some mountains, until the army had passed them; that Colonel Butler promised he would send back some warriors, who should conduct them by bye-ways to some place of safety. She further adds, that, previous to the squaws going off, there was great contention with them and the warriors about their going off; the former had determined on staying and submitting to our generosity; the latter opposed it, and informed them that, by such a step, the Americans would be able to bring them to any terms they pleased; whereas, did they go off, they would have it in their power to come to more favourable terms, should a treaty of any kind be offered.

Catharines town is pleasantly situated on a creek, about three miles from Seneca Lake; it contained nearly fifty houses, in general, very good — the country near is very excellent. We found several very fine corn-fields, which afforded the greatest plenty of corn, beans, &c., of which, after our fatiguing march, we had an agreeable repast. After getting everything in perfect readiness, we took up our line of march at 7 o'clock this morning. The roads from this place for about one mile were rather difficult and swampy. We then ascended a rising country, which was, in general, level, excepting a few defiles which we had to pass, but were by no reason dangerous or difficult. The lands are rich, abounding with fine, large, and clear timber, chiefly white oak, hickory, walnut, and ash; bounded on the left for about three miles with excellent marsh or meadow ground, after which proceeds the beautiful Seneca lake, which abounds with all kinds of fish, particularly salmon, trout, rock, that which resembles perch, as also sheep-head.

Previous to our leaving this place, the squaw which was taken here, was left, and a hut erected, of which she took possession, A quantity of wood was also gathered and carried to the hut for her use; she was also provided with a quantity of provisions. All these favours had such an effect on her that it drew tears from her savage eyes.

It is about three miles in breadth, and about forty miles in length. Upon the right, though considerably up the country, is another delightful lake, called Kayuga Lake; abounds with all kinds of fish also, and is about forty-six miles in length.

We proceeded along this beautiful country about twelve miles, and encamped near a corn-field, on which stood several Indian cabins; bearing between the light corps and main army an advantageous ravine, and, bounded on our left by Seneca lake.

Previous to our arrival here the Indians who occupied the cabins already mentioned, probably discovered our approach, pushed off precipitately, leaving their kettles with corn boiling over the fire. During our march this day we discovered several trees with the following characters newly cut on them by those savages commanded by Brandt and the Butlers, and with whom we had the action on the 29th ultimo.

Saturday, Sept. 4th. — On account of the rain this morning the array did not move until 10 o'clock, A. M. We passed through a delightful level country, the soil of which very rich, the timber fine and large, interspersed with hazel bushes, fine grass and pea vines. On our march we discovered several fires burning, which fully intimated some of the savages were not far off in front of us. We destroyed several fields of corn, and, after a march of thirteen miles, we encamped in the woods, in the front of a very large ravine, and about half a mile from Seneca Lake. On account of some difficulties with the pack-horses, &c., the main army did not reach so far as the infantry, and encamped about two miles in their rear.

Sunday, Sept. 5th. — About 9 o'clock this morning the army moved through a country much the same as yesterday. About 12 o'clock we arrived at Canadia, about three miles from the last encampment, where we encamped for this night. Previous to our arrival we entered several corn-fields, and furnished the men with two days allowance of the same. The riflemen, who were advanced, retook a prisoner who was taken last year by the savages on the east branch of the Susquehanna. An Indian, who lay concealed, fired, but without effect on our riflemen, and immediately fled.

Oil examining this prisoner, he informed us that Brandt, with near a thousand savages, including Butler's Rangers, left this town last Friday, seemingly much frightened and fatigued — that they were pushing for Kanadauaga, and Indian village, where they mean to make a stand and give us battle. He further informs us that, exclusive of a considerable number of savages killed and wounded in the action of the 29th, seven Tories were killed; that all their wounded, with some dead, were carried in Canoes up the Cayuga branch — that they allow they sustained a very heavy loss in that action.

Canadia is much the finest village we have yet come to. It is situated on a rising ground, in the midst of an extensive apple and peach orchard, within half a mile of Seneca Lake; it contains about forty well-finished houses, and everything about it seems neat and well improved.

Monday, Sept. 6th. — The fore part of the day was entirely employed in hunting up our horses and cattle, a number of which were lost. About 2 o'clock we took up our line of march, and moved about three miles, where we encamped on a beautiful piece of woodland, (interspersed with vast quantities of pea vines, which served for food for our horses,) our rear covered by the lake, our flank by considerable ravines.

On the fourth, whilst on our march, several officers' waiters, who had delayed in the rear, lost the path along which the army moved, and, towards night, found themselves near an Indian village, which had been previously evacuated. They found a quantity of plunder, which they brought off, first putting the town in flames. A captain and a party, on missing, being sent in pursuit, and fell in with them as they were returning to the encamping place occupied by the army the preceding day, and conducted them safe to the army at Canadia.

An express from Tioga, with packets, &c., for the army, arrived this day at head quarters — received several letters from my friends.

Tuesday, Sept. 7th. — At half-past seven o'clock the army moved and arrived at the head of the lake about 2 o'clock, P. M. The country we passed through was exceedingly fine, and chiefly along the water for eight miles and a half.

About 3 o'clock, P. M., the rifle and infantry corps crossed at the mouth of the lake, about knee deep, and not above thirty yards wide. On our arrival on the opposite shore, we immediately entered a dangerous and narrow defile, bounded on the left by the head of Seneca Lake, and on our right by a large morass and flooded at intervals, well calculated to form an ambuscade. From every circumstance, both as to intelligence and the great advantage the enemy might have had from its situation, we fairly expected an attack. However, we moved through in files, supported by the two flanking divisions, and gained the other side. The main army then crossed, and took our place. We then moved through a second defile, as difficult as the first, and formed again until the main army possessed themselves of the same ground we had just left. We then marched and passed a third defile, and formed in a corn-field, near a large house, which was beautifully situated on the head of the lake, and generally occupied by Butler, one of the savage leaders.

The light corps, flanked by two flanking divisions, received orders to move and gain the rear of the town. The main army took the path, and marched immediately in front of the same; but the enemy no doubt having previous notice of our movements, had abandoned the town, which we entered about dusk, leaving behind them a number of bear and deer skins, and also a fine white child of about three years old.

This town is called Kanadasaga, and appears to be one of their capital settlements; about it is a fine apple orchard and a council-house. There was in the neighbourhood a great quantity of corn, beans, &c., which, after taking great quantities for the use of the army, we totally destroyed; burned the houses, which were in number about fifty, and girdled the apple trees. Distance of march this day, about 12 miles.

Wednesday, Sept. 8th. — This day we lay on our ground; the rifle corps, with several other parties, were detached down the lake to destroy a small village, called Gaghsiungua, and a quantity of corn, &c., in this neighbourhood, and the army prepared for a march early to-morrow morning.

Various opinions prevailed between many officers about our proceeding any further on account of our provisions; but General Sullivan, with a number of officers, nobly resolved to encounter every difficulty to execute the important expedition, and determined, notwithstanding the horrid neglect in not furnishing us with provision, horses, &c., sufficient to enable us to carry through the expedition, even to proceed on with the scanty pittance, and accomplish the arduous task of destroying the whole Seneca country.

Thursday, Sept. 9th. — On account of a number of pack horses which had gone astray and could not be found, the army did not march at 6 o'clock agreeable to yesterday's orders. A command of fifty men, under a captain, returned from this place to Tioga to escort the sick and those who were not able to proceed without retarding the march of the army, which is now under the necessity on account of our wants to be as expeditious as possible to complete the expedition; all those pack horses which were lame, or otherwise reduced, likewise returned.

About twelve o'clock the army marched; their first route was over bushy land, interspersed with remarkably wild high grass, and appeared to have been formerly cleared. We then descended into an extensive maple swamp, which was very rich, and well calculated for meadow. After marching seven miles, we came to a creek, known by the name of Flint Creek, which the whole, excepting Clinton's brigade, crossed, and encamped on a plain which had been occupied by the enemy but a few days before for the same purpose. Distance of march, seven miles.

The rifle corps who yesterday went to destroy Gaghsiungua this evening returned. They report it was a fine town, well improved, with a great quantity of corn near the same; likewise, an abundance of beans, watermelons, peaches, and all kinds of vegetables, the whole of which they totally destroyed.

Friday, Sept. 10th. — At 8 o'clock this morning the army took up their line of march in the usual order. Their route, about four miles, continued through the swamp, which, in some places, was miry, and difficult for pack horses, otherwise the foot would not have been much retarded. We then arrived on very fine ground for marching, which, to all appearance, was old cleared fields, as they contained a great quantity of wild grass as high as the horses in many places. The land continued in this manner (alternately having a strip of wood between) for about four miles, when we arrived at a lake, (the name I could not learn,) which appeared to be a mile wide, and six or seven miles in length. We marched half a mile along this lake, and came to the mouth, which we crossed; the water was not knee deep, and about thirty yards over; but it narrowed so fast that, about twenty yards from the mouth, it was not in width more than five, but much deeper. We then moved up a fine country from the lake, and in half a mile came to Kanadalaugua, a beautifully situated town, containing between twenty and thirty houses, well finished, chiefly of hewn plank, which we immediately burned, and pro- ceeded about half a mile on our right, where we found a large field of corn, squashes, beans, &c. At this place we en- camped, but were very badly off for water, having none but what we sent half a mile for, and that very bad. The Seneca country, from its extreme flatness, having no good springs, which is extremely disagreeable for a marching army. Distance of march this day, 9 miles.

In this town a dog was hung up, with a string of wampum round his neck, on a tree, curiously decorated and trimmed. On inquiry, I was informed that it was a custom among the savages before they went to war to offer this as a sacrifice to Mars, the God of War, and praying that he might strengthen them. In return for those favours, they promise to present him with the skin for a tobacco pouch.

Saturday, Sept. 11th. — Agreeable to orders we took up our line of march this morning precisely at 6 o'clock. We moved through a thicket and swamp near one mile before we gained the main path. The infantry, on account of this difficult swamp, could not possibly march in the usual order, without being considerably dispersed. We moved along this path for about three miles, after which we ascended a rising ground; the country remarkably fine and rich, covered chiefly with pine, oak, and hickory timber. At intervals we crossed considerable clear fields, with remarkably high, wild grass. About 1 o'clock we descended into a most beautiful valley, within one mile of an Indian village, known by the name of Anyayea, situate on a fine plain, within about half a mile of Anyayea Lake, which is but small and very beautiful, and abounds with all kinds of fish. This town contains about twelve houses, chiefly hewn logs. About it are several large corn-fields, and a number of apple and other fruit trees. We encamped about two o'clock for this day, after completing a march of thirteen miles.

Sunday, Sept. 12th. — In order to expedite our march, and prevent the enemy from making off with their effects from Jenese, their capital, and last town in the Seneca country, it was determined a garrison of fifty men, with those soldiers who were not very able to march, should continue at this post, in order to guard our stores, viz., ammunition, and flour, until our return.

The rain having set in very heavy this morning, we could not move until about twelve o'clock. We then began our march, but, on account of a defile which we had to cross, could not march in the usual order. After passing the same, we took up our line of march as usual, and ascended a rising piece of ground. After marching about five miles, we came to a lake, which we crossed at the mouth, being about knee deep, and about ten yards over. We then ascended another rising piece of ground, composed of exceedingly fine, rich land, with large oak and hickory timber, and, at intervals, with marsh or swamp, well calculated for meadow ground. After arriving within half a mile of Kanaghsas, a small Indian village, which was previously destined for this day's march, night set in, and the main army being at least a mile in our rear, we received orders to encamp for this night, which was in the woods, and exceedingly ill calculated for that purpose, no water being nearer than half a mile. This day's march completed twelve miles.

After we encamped, Lieutenant Boyd, of the rifle corps, some volunteers, and as many riflemen, made up six and twenty in the whole, were sent up to reconnoitre the town of Jenesse, having for their guide an Oneida Indian, named Hanyost, a chief of that tribe, who has been remarkable for his attachment to this country, having served as a volunteer since the commencement of the war.

Monday, Sept, 13th. — This morning before daylight we left; the general beat, on which the tents were immediately struck, and in half an hour the army marched into the town of Kanaghsas, which contained ten houses, situate on a flat near the head of a small lake. The flat contained a great quantity of corn, and vegetables of all kinds, which were remarkably well tended. At this place we halted to draw provisions, viz., beef, (half allowance,) and to destroy the town, corn, &c.

Four men of Lieutenant Boyd's party this morning returned, bringing information of the town of Gaghsuquilahery (which they took for Jenese) being abandoned. About 12 o'clock we were alarmed by some Indians firing and giving chase to Mr. Lodge and a few men who went forward to survey. They wounded a corporal, who died next day, and chased them until one of our camp sentinels fired on them and stopped their career.

Lieutenant Boyd having retired from the town of Gaghsuquilahery to wait for the arrival of the main army, which was detained longer than he expected, he sent back two men to know the cause; these two men had not gone far before they discovered a few Indians ahead. They then retired and informed Lieutenant Boyd, who immediately, with his party, gave chase, and followed them within about two miles and a half from the main army, where a body of savages, of at least four or five hundred, lay concealed, and probably intended giving the main army (the ground being favourable on their side) a fire, and push off according to custom, who immediately surrounded him and his party. He nobly fought them for some considerable time; but, by their great superiority, he was obliged to attempt a retreat, at the same time loading and firing as his party ran.

The Indians killed, and in the most inhuman manner, tomahawked and scalped six that were found. Nine of the party have got safe in; but Lieutenant Boyd and Henjost, (the Indian already mentioned,) with seven others, are yet missing, one of whom we know is a prisoner, as one Murphy, a rifleman of the party, who made his escape, saw him in their possession. This Murphy is a noted marksman, and a great soldier, he having billed and scalped that morning, in the town they were at, an Indian, which makes the three and thirtieth man of the enemy he has killed, as is well known to his officers, this war.

There being a swamp or morass totally impassable for our horses, in front of Kanaghsas, the infantry and rifle corps passed over, and ascended the hill, wherein Indians lay, in hopes to come up with them; but they had fled, leaving behind them upwards of one hundred blankets, a great number of hats, and many other things, which we took, and then halted until the main army arrived, they having first been obliged, in order to enable them to move, to throw a hedge over the morass.

The whole then took up their line of march, and proceeded to the town of Gaghsuquilahery, through the finest country I almost ever saw, without exception. Before dusk we arrived within sight of the town. The Indians, having thrown themselves in a wood on the opposite side, the following disposition for an attack was immediately ordered to take place, viz.: The infantry, with the artillery, to push on in front ; General Maxwell's brigade, with the left flanking division, to endeavour to gain the enemy's right ; General Poor's brigade to move and gain their left; the right flanking division, and two regiments from General Clinton's brigade to move round Poor's right flank; the infantry to rush on in front, supported by the remainder of Clinton's brigade. We then moved forward, and took possession of the town without opposition, the enemy flying before us across a branch of Genese river, through a thicket, where it was impossible for us to follow, we not being acquainted with the country, and night having set in. We received orders to encamp, after making a march of eight and a half miles.

Tuesday, Sept. 14th. — Previous to our march this morning parties were ordered out to destroy the corn, which they did, plucking and throwing it into the river. About 11 o'clock we took up our line of march and proceeded for Jenese, the last and capital settlement of the Seneca country; the whole crossed a branch of the Jenise river, and moved through a considerable swamp, and formed on a plain the other side, the most extensive I ever saw, containing not less than six thousand acres of the richest soil that can be conceived, not having a bush standing, but filled with grass considerably higher than a man. We moved up this plain for about three miles in our regular line of march, which was a beautiful site, as a view of the whole could be had at one look, and then came to Jenise river, which we crossed, being about forty yards over, and near middle deep, and then ascended a rising ground, which afforded a prospect which was so beautiful that, to attempt a comparison, would be doing an injury, as we had a view as far as our eyes could carry us of another plain, besides the one we crossed, through which the Jenise river formed a most beautiful winding, and, at intervals, cataracts, which rolled from the rocks, and emptied into the river.

We then marched on through a rough but rich country, until we arrived at the capital town, which is much the largest we have yet met with in our whole route, and encamped about the same.

At this place we found the body of the brave but unfortunate Lieutenant Boyd, and one rifleman, massacred in the most cruel and barbarous manner that the human mind can possibly conceive; the savages having put them to the most excruciating torments possible, by first plucking their nails from their hands, then spearing, cutting, and whipping them, and mangling their bodies, then cutting off the flesh from their shoulders by pieces, tomahawking and severing their heads from their bodies, and then leaving them a prey to their dogs. We likewise found one house burned, in which, probably, was a scene as cruel as the former.

This evening the remains of Lieutenant Boyd and the rifleman's corpse were interred with military honours. Mr. Boyd's former good character, as a brave soldier, and an

honest man, and his behaviour in the skirmish of yesterday (several of the Indians being found dead, and some seen carried off,) must endear him to all friends of mankind. May his fate await those who have been the cause of his. Oh! Britain, behold and blush. Jenise town, the capital of the Seneca nation, is pleasantly situated on a rich and extensive flat, the soil remarkably rich, and great parts well improved with fields of corn, beans, potatoes, and all kinds of vegetables. It contained one hundred and seven well-finished houses.

Wednesday, Sept. 15th. — This morning the whole army, excepting a covering party, were engaged in destroying the corn, beans, potatoes, and other vegetables, which were in quantity immense, and in goodness unequaled by any I ever yet saw. Agreeable to a moderate calculation, there was not less than two hundred acres, the whole of which was pulled and piled up in large heaps, mixed with dry wood, taken from the houses, and consumed to ashes. About 3 o'clock, P. M., the business was finished, and the immediate objects of this expedition completed, viz., the total ruin of the Indian settlements, and the destruction of their crops. The following is a part of the orders issued this day, viz.:

"The commander-in-chief informs this brave and resolute army that the immediate objects of this expedition are accomplished, viz.: total ruin of the Indian settlements, and the destruction of their crops, which were designed for the support of those inhuman barbarians, while they were desolating the American frontiers. He is by no means insensible of the obligations he is under to those brave officers and soldiers whose virtue and fortitude have enabled him to complete the important design of the expedition, and he assures them he will not fail to inform America at large how much they stand indebted to them. The army will this day commence its march for Tioga."

Previous to our leaving Jenise, a woman with a child came in to us, who had been taken prisoner last year near Wyoming, and fortunately made her escape from the savages. She, with her bantling, was almost starved for want of food; she informs us that the Indians have been in great want all last spring — that they subsisted entirely on green corn this summer— that their squaws were fretting prodigiously, and continually teasing their warriors to make peace — that by promises by Butler and his minions, they are fed up with great things that should be done for them— that they seem considerably cast down and frightened; and, in short, she says distress and trouble seem painted on their countenances. Distance of march this day, six miles.

Thursday, Sept. 16th. — After destroying several corn-fields, we took up our line of march about 11 o'clock, A. M., and proceeded towards Kanaghsas. Previous to our arrival there, parties were ordered out to reconnoitre the woods, and gather the bodies of those soldiers who fell in the skirmish of the 13th. Fourteen, including those six mentioned in my journal of the 13th, were found, and buried with military honours. The sight was most shocking, as they were all scalped, tomahawked, and most inhumanly mangled. Amongst those unfortunate men was Hanjost, the volunteer Indian, who fared equally with the rest. About six o'clock we arrived at Kanaghsas, and encamped. We found several corn-fields, which were immediately laid waste. Our march this day, 9 miles.

Friday, Sept. 17th. — About 5 o'clock this morning the

general beat, the tents were struck, and the line of march taken up about 6 o'clock. We arrived at Anyeaya about 12 o'clock, being the place our stores, with a garrison, was left. It was not with a little satisfaction that we found everything safe. We were not without our apprehensions about them, on account of the intelligence we were fearful the enemy might have collected from the unfortunate prisoners who fell in their hands on the 13th. We encamped in the same order and on the same ground as on the 11th inst.

Saturday, Sept. 18th. — This morning about 8 o'clock the army moved; the rear was ordered (before they left the ground) to kill all such horses as were unable to move along, lest they should fall into the enemy's hands. On our route we fell in with several Oneida Indians, (our friends,) who seemed much rejoiced at our great success against the Seneca nations. We arrived about 6 o'clock, P. M., at the east side of the Kanadaugua Lake, where we encamped, after completing a march of thirteen miles and a half.

Sunday, Sept. 19th. — The army moved at eight o'clock this morning in the usual order; — excepting a few obstructions they met with passing through several swamps, they marched remarkably steady. On our route we were met by an express from Tioga, who brought a number of letters and papers informing us of Spain declaring war against Great Britain. They also brought us the agreeable intelligence of a good supply for the army having come on to Newtown, (about twenty miles above Tioga,) to meet us. This agreeable intelligence conspired to make us exceedingly happy, as we had not only been a long time entirely in the dark with respect to home news, but the disagreeable reflection of half allowance was entirely dispelled.

We pursued our march until we arrived at Kanadasaga, which was about dusk. When the infantry got up; we encamped on the same ground, and in the same position, as on the 7th, after completing a march of fifteen miles.

Monday, Sept. 20th. — The greater part of the day was employed at head-quarters in holding a council in consequence of the intercession made by some Oneida Indians, (our friends) in favour of the Cayuga tribe, who have been for some time past in alliance with the Senecas, and acted with them, and are now desirous to make peace with us. The council determined no treaty should be held with them, and a command of five hundred infantry, with Major Parr's rifle corps, were immediately detached and sent to Cayuga Lake, on which their settlement lay, with orders to lay wait and destroy their towns, corn, &c., and receive none of them but in the characters of prisoners of war. Col. Smith, with two hundred men, was also dispatched down the north side of the Seneca lake in order to finish the destruction of Gausiunque, an Indian village about eight miles below Canadasaga. Colonel Gainsworth, with one hundred men, was likewise detached, and sent to Fort Stanwix for some business, from whence he is to proceed to head-quarters on the north river, and join the main army.

About 4 o'clock, P. M., the array took up their line of march, and moved steadily. About half-past five they reached and crossed the outlet of Seneca lake, and encamped about one mile beyond the same.

Tuesday, Sept. 21st. — The army marched this morning about eight o'clock, and continued moving steadily until we passed Canadia about two miles, where we encamped, near the lake. Previous to our marching this morning. Colonel Dearbourn, with a command of two hundred men, marched to destroy a town on the north side of Cayuga Lake. Distance of march this day, 13 miles.

Thursday, Sept. 23d. — About 8 o'clock this morning the army marched, and arrived at Catharines town about 2 o'clock, P. M., where we made a small halt. We found at this place the old Indian squaw who was left here on our march up the country. General Sullivan gave her a considerable supply of flour and meat, for which, with tears in her savage eyes, she expressed a great deal of thanks. During our absence from this place a young squaw came and attended on the old one; but some inhuman villain who passed through killed her. What made this crime still more heinous was, because a manifesto was left with the old squaw positively forbidding any violence or injury should be committed on the women or children of the savages, by virtue of which it appears this young squaw came to this place, which absolutely comes under the virtue of a breach of faith, and the offender ought to be severely punished.

I went to view, in company with a number of gentlemen, a very remarkable fall of water, which is about one mile above this place. Its beauty and elegance surpass almost anything I ever saw. The fall is not less than two hundred feet. About 3 o'clock the army moved about three miles further, and encamped on a plain at the entrance of the great swamp, after completing a march of thirteen miles and a half.

Friday, Sept. 24th. — This morning precisely at 8 o'clock the army moved, and continued their route through the hemlock swamp mentioned in the 1st inst., meeting with much fewer obstructions than we expected, owing to the very dry weather which we have had for this month past. After passing through the same we came to a fine open country, and soon arrived at Kanawaluhery, where there was a post established with a reinforcement of stores, which was a most pleasing circumstance, as the last was issued, and that at half allowance, at Kanadaraga. On our arrival, the garrison saluted with the discharge of thirteen cannon, which compliment was returned them by the array.

Saturday, Sept. 25th. — In consequence of the accession of the King of Spain to the American alliance, and the generous proceedings of the present Congress in augmenting the subsistence of the officers and men of the army, General Sullivan ordered five head of the best cattle, viz.: one for the use of the officers of each brigade, with five gallons of spirits each, to be delivered to them respectively, thereby giving them an opportunity of testifying their joy on this occasion.

In the evening, the whole was drawn up and fired a feu-de-joie, thirteen cannon being first discharged. The infantry then commenced a running fire through the whole line, which, being repeated a second time, the whole army gave three cheers, viz., one for the United States of America, one for Congress, and one for our new ally, the King of Spain.

The army being then dismissed. General Hand, with the officers of his brigade, attended by the officers of the park or artillery, repaired to a bowery, erected for that purpose, where the fatted bullock was served up, (dressed in different ways,) the whole seated themselves on the ground around the same, which afforded them a most agreeable repast. The officers being very jovial, and the evening was spent in great mirth and jollity.

After dinner the following toasts were drank, the drums and fifes playing at intervals.

1st. The thirteen states and their sponsors.
2d. The honourable, the American Congress.
3d. General Washington and the American army.
4th. The commander-in-chief of the western expedition.

5th. The American navy.

6th. Our faithful allies, the united houses of Bourbon.

7th. May the American Congress, and all her legislative representatives, be endowed with virtue and wisdom, and may her independence be as firmly established as the pillars of time.

8th. May the citizens of America, and her soldiers, be ever unanimous in the reciprocal support of each other.

9th. May altercations, discord, and every degree of fraud, be totally banished the peaceful shores of America.

10th. May the memory of the brave Lieutenant Boyd, and the soldiers under his command, who were horribly massacred by the inhuman savages, or by their more barbarous and detestable allies, the British and Tories, on the 13th inst., be ever dear to his country.

11th. An honourable peace with America, or perpetual war with her enemies.

12th. May the kingdom of Ireland merit a stripe in the American standard.

13th. May the enemies of America be metamorphosed into pack horses, and sent on a western expedition against the Indians.

An express, with dispatches for General Sullivan, from Philadelphia, arrived this morning, by whom I received a packet enclosing the commissions for my officers.

About 11 o'clock, A. M., the command under Colonel Dearbourn, who left us the 21st of June to proceed to Cayuga lake, returned, bringing two squaw prisoners; he having, in his route, destroyed several towns and a great quantity of fine corn.

Monday, Sept. 27th. — The detachment ordered to march yesterday moved this morning up Tioga branch to an Indian village, about twelve miles from this place, with orders to destroy the same.

Coleman and Caldwell, two of my soldiers, who, by some means, lost the regiment at Kanadaugua lake, on the eighteenth, after wandering for seven days in the wilderness, found and joined us at this place. They subsisted, during their absence, on the hearts and livers of two dead horses which they found on the path along which the army had marched.

At dusk this evening, the detachment which marched this morning returned, after destroying a considerable quantity of corn, beans, and other vegetables, sixteen boat loads of which they brought with them for the use of the army ; they also burned a small village.

Tuesday, Sept. 28th. — Several commands were ordered out this day, viz., one up and the other down the Tioga branch, for the purpose of destroying corn, &c., of which there was a quantity left on our march towards the Seneca country.

All the lame and sick soldiers of the army were this day ordered to go to Tioga in boats, and the pack horses least able for other duty.

Colonel Butler, with his command, after laying waste and destroying the Cayuga settlements, and corn, &c., of which there Was a very great quantity, returned, and joined the army about 10 o'clock this morning.

Wednesday, Sept. 29th — The army marched this morning about 8 o'clock, and continued moving steadily until we passed Chemung about one mile, where we encamped on the same ground, and in the same position, as on the

27th. The two commands ordered out yesterday morning returned, and joined the army at this place about 9 o'clock, P. M., after destroying large quantities of corn, beans, and other vegetables.

Thursday, Sept. 30th. — This morning about 8 o'clock the army moved. About 2 o'clock they arrived at Tioga plains, near Fort Sullivan, where the whole formed in regular line of march, and moved into the garrison in the greatest order, when we were received with military honours, the garrison turning out with presented arms, and a salute of thirteen rounds from their artillery, which complement was returned them from the park of artillery with the army.

Colonel Shrieve, governor of the garrison, had an elegant dinner provided for the general and field officers of the army. We regaled ourselves, and great joy and good humour was visible in every countenance. Colonel Proctor's band, and drums and fifes played in concert the whole time.

Friday, Oct. 1st. — This morning the horses belonging to the officers of the brigade were forwarded to Wyoming. We also sent our cow which we had along with us the whole expedition, and to whom we are under infinite obligations for the great quantity of milk she afforded us, which rendered our situation very comfortable, and was no small addition to our half allowance.

This afternoon Colonel Brewer, General Sullivan's secretary, set off to Congress with the dispatches, which contained a relation of the great success of the expedition.

Saturday, Oct. 2d. — This day the commander-in-chief made an elegant entertainment, and invited all the general and field officers of the army to dine with him.

In the evening, to conclude the mirth of the day, we had an Indian dance. The officers who joined in it putting on vizors, (alias Monetas.) The dance was conducted and led off by a young Sachem of the Oneida tribe, who was next followed by several other Indians, then the whole led off, and, after the Indian custom, danced to the music, which was a rattle, a knife, and a pipe, which the Sachem continued clashing together and singing Indian the whole time. At the end of each, the Indian whoop was set up by the whole.

Sunday, Oct. 3d. — Agreeable to the orders of yesterday, the garrison of Fort Sullivan this day joined their respective corps, and the fort was demolished. The stores and other baggage with the park of artillery were put on board the boats, and every other matter put in perfect readiness to move with the army, on their route to Wyoming, to-morrow morning at 6 o'clock.

The young Sachem, with several Oneida Indians, relatives and friends of the unfortunate Indian Hanjost, who bravely fell with the party under command of the much lamented Lieut. Boyd on the 13th ult., who faithfully acted as guide to the army, left us this day, well pleased, (after bestowing some presents on them,) for their native place, the Oneida country.

The German regiment, which composed a part of the flanking divisions of the army, was this day ordered to join and do duty with the third Pennsylvania brigade, commanded by Gen. Hand.

Monday, Oct. 4th. — This day about 8 o'clock the army took up their line of March. We arrived at Wesauking about 6 o'clock in the evening, after completing a march of fifteen miles. On account of the rain, marching was rather disagreeable this day.

On my arrival at this place I received a letter, with some newspapers, &c., from his excellency, President Read, which contained agreeable news, &c.

Wednesday, Oct. 6th. — About 8 o'clock this morning the whole embarked again, and moved, paying no attention to order down the river.

Thursday, Oct. 7th. — Embarked about 6 o'clock, and kept on steadily until we arrived at Wyoming. About 3 o'clock, P. M., the whole army landed and encamped on the same ground, and in the same order, as on the 30th of July.

Thus, by the perseverance, good conduct, and determined resolution of our commander-in-chief, with the assistance of his council, and the full determination of his troops to execute, have we fully accomplished the great end and intentions of this important expedition; and I flatter myself we fully surpassed the most sanguine expectations of those whose eyes were more immediately looking to us for success.

The glorious achievements we have exhibited in extending our conquests so far, and. at the same time, render them so very complete, will make no inconsiderable balance even in the present politics of America, Its future good consequences I leave to the eloquence of time to declare, which will, in ages hence, celebrate the memory of those brave sons who nobly risked their livés, disdaining every fatigue and hardship, to complete a conquest, the real good effects and advantages of which posterity will particularly enjoy.

Whilst I revere the merit and virtue of the army, I am sorry I am under the necessity of mentioning that there was an unparalleled and unpardonable neglect, (and which ought not to pass with impunity,) in those whose business it was to supply them with a sufficient quantity of necessaries to carry them through the expedition, instead of which not more than twenty-two days flour, and sixteen days meat was on hand when it commenced. And, although the army possessed a degree of virtue, perhaps unparalleled in the annals of history, in undertaking an expedition on half allowance, which was in every instance hazardous and imperious, yet, had we not been favored with the smiles of Providence, in a continuation of good weather, the half allowance itself would not have enabled us to perform what, from that circumstance, we have.

THE END.

Other New York military books
from New York History Review

*A Soldier's Story: Prison Life and Other Incidents
in the War of 1861-1865 - Elmira Prison Camp*
by Miles O. Sherrill

*To War and Back - Carl Albert Janowski's
Army Diary 1918-1919*

*In Their Honor - Soldiers of the Confederacy -
The Elmira Prison Camp*
by Diane Janowski

Diary of A Tar Heel Confederate Soldier
by L. Leon

*The Elmira Prison Camp, a History of the Military Prison
at Elmira, New York July 6, 1864 - July 10, 1865
with New Appendix*
by Clay Holmes

www.ingramcontent.com/pod-product-compliance
Lightning Source LLC
Chambersburg PA
CBHW021021090426
42738CB00007B/862